MY DREAM GREEN ORB

WHERE BUSINESS MEETS THE PLANET'S NEEDS

by anindita ghosh

INDIA · SINGAPORE · MALAYSIA

ISBN 979-8-89744-251-5

DISCLAIMER

The content of this book, including case studies, examples, and data points, draws from publicly available information as of 2024. While extensive research has been conducted to ensure accuracy, the field of sustainability and corporate environmental initiatives is rapidly evolving. The company names, trademarks, statistics, and initiatives mentioned throughout the book are the property of their respective owners and have been cited from public sources including annual reports, company websites, press releases, and verified news articles.

This book presents an independent analysis and perspective on business sustainability. No company, organization, or entity mentioned has endorsed this work or its contents. The transformation stories, statistics, and examples are compiled from public records and are used solely for educational and illustrative purposes. The author has no direct affiliation with these organizations.

The recommendations, strategies, and insights provided are meant to serve as general guidance for businesses considering sustainable transformation. Readers should conduct their own due diligence and consult appropriate professionals before implementing any suggestions. The author and publisher make no representations or warranties regarding the accuracy, completeness, or timeliness of the information contained herein and assume no responsibility for any decisions made based on this content.

This book is dedicated to my Father,

My quiet hero, my steady guide.

You've taught me to see the world with patience and care,

To learn from my mistakes and grow with each step.

Thank you for always being my light.

CONTENTS

Preface   *11*

Introduction   *15*

Part 1: The Wake Up   **17**

Chapter 1   The Price We Never Meant to Pay   19

Chapter 2   The Footprints We Cannot See   27

Part 2: Reimagining Business   **37**

Chapter 3   Nature's Blueprint   39

Chapter 4   The Green Revolution in
                       the Boardroom   53

Chapter 5   Tomorrow's Tools Today   65

Part 3: The Green Epilogue **73**

Chapter 6   Breaking Through the Barriers   75

Chapter 7   The Green Orb: Your Turn   85

Dismantling few Myths That Cloud Our Green Vision   *99*

Carbon Footprint Reduction Guide:
From Quick Wins to Transformative Impact   *105*

References   *111*

Acknowledgments   *115*

About the Author   *117*

PREFACE

When the monsoon's first raindrops fall on the earth's surface, it releases a pleasant earthy smell. This is one of my earliest cherished memories. As a kid, I used to stand on the balcony and see the rain falling, and the earth started turning to dark. The leaves are getting clean, and all of a sudden the atmosphere feels more alive. My favorite season remains the same though it is winter.

Why I am telling these experiences is one of the reasons behind writing this book, expressing my thoughts. My interest in knowing the nature, spending time with it started early as just another kid. When growing up geography as a subject also fascinates me. I started capturing the beauty of nature in my drawings and as images on phone. I feel connected to the mountains, forests, rivers, air, moon, birds, and every creation of the nature. I feel they all have a story of years and years of existence. While learning about them more and more I started understanding the nature's perfect systems. Their imperfection and sustainable in their complexity seem perfect to me.

But as I grew older, after getting senses to understand the world around me, like over the past 15 years or so, I began to notice some disconnection. The stories of nature that I have heard from my father, from my grandmother, compared to what I saw as a kid and now what I see, a lot in this nature have changed. The stars in the night sky are now barely visible, the small streams of water are now polluted.

Where I live there is a steel plant and a thermal power station too. You can smell a burn or chemically smell in the air, also the rooftops are covered with a thin black dust layer. The huge trees which once used to be a landmark, those huge trunks are now not there. I barely see a sparrow now which once use to come at our home's ventilators.

Yes, a lot got changed, and that's sad, this realization of losing the nature is sad. But I am hopeful that many people, companies, organizations, etc, are realizing this change, waking up to this reality and strated making changes.

We all are involved in this, making the nature look like what it is today. But in this book I have expressed the role of our businesses' involvement in changing our very nature's landscape which sustain us. I have expressed my realization and probable solutions for businesses, how they hold an immense power to change the world back again what it was years back.

I don't have years of experience though, but I have spent hours reading academic research papers, environmental case studies, public articles, books, documentaries, personal observations, etc. All of this has shaped my thinking and this book. Having a business background I have tried to look at this problem from the lens of business point of view, like what we have done wrong, what we are still doing wrong and what can be the solutions.

Through the chapters you will feel the flow of realization, understanding, solutions and the future we want to see (My Dream Green Orb). I hope this book will give a bit of understanding between business and nature, profit and preservation, etc. For the young ones reading this, I hope you'll find inspiration in nature's brilliant creations. For every business, I hope these pages will offer pathways of thought and action by which we can feel the nature as it was.

We are standing at a crucial juncture in human history and our decisions today will echo through future generations. The message remains clear throughout the chapters, which is Build with the nature, not against it. The journey to that dream planet is not so easy, but now it is necessary maybe if we don't take action today after a few decades it will be too late.

This is my first book, I have poured my heart into it. If there are any errors or shortcomings, I apologize for them; they are entirely mine. But I hope the message shines through clear and strong. Thank you.

Anindita Ghosh

Durgapur

14th Feb 2025

INTRODUCTION

৶৶

In this era of human progress, we are at an interesting intersection where business ambition meets environmental imperative. This book is an exploration of how the businesses can become a catalyst for the ecological renewal.

The title "My Dream Green Orb" comes from a realization that: our planet is not just a resource that we need to manage but it has emotions, it is a living sphere which holds our dreams. As you go through the chapters you will find that it is not a manifesto or a collection of eco friendly practices. It is how we can reimagine the business while taking care of our nature.

The chapters are structured in three distinct phases. First, we confront the uncomfortable truth of how traditional business practices harm our planet. Then we will find the unique ways to approach particular problems, and finally we will envision our green world through the businesses

There are lots of real world practical examples from startups to multinational corporations, from local initiatives to global movements. We will follow the proven pathways of nature and write our green story together.

This book is an invitation to think differently, and consistently. A true call to recognize the every decision we make, we product we create, and every policy we implement has a ripple on the world around us. This journey is about progress not perfection. We are a part of this largest ecosystem and in long term our success is directly proportional to the health of our planet.

As you turn these pages, I hope you feel inspired not just by the ideas but by the possibility of what we can achieve together. This is not just my dream, it is our shared vision for a GreenOrb, a world where businesses grow in harmony with nature. Let us begin this journey with humility, generosity, and the belief that even the smallest steps can lead to profound change.

PART 1: THE WAKE UP

EARTH'S INVOICE

Invoice to :

Humans

Invoice No :   Date Issued :   **Planet Earth**
#00-00001   2024

Atmosphere

Air Quality	**HAZARDOUS**
Ozone Layer	**THINNING**
Greenhouse Gases	**CRITICAL**
Clean Air	**DEPLETING**

Oceans & Waters

Ocean Health	**DETERIORATING**
Marine Life	**ENDANGERED**
Coral Reefs	**BLEACHING**
Fresh Water	**CONTAMINATED**
Glaciers	**MELTING**

Living Systems

Biodiversity	**COLLAPSING**
Wildlife	**VANISHING**
Forests	**SHRINKING**
Soil Health	**DEGRADING**
Pollinators	**DECLINING**

Urban Environment

Heat Islands	**INTENSIFYING**
Urban Air Quality	**TOXIC**
Green Corridors	**DIMINISHING**
Noise Pollution	**RISING**
Light Pollution	**INCREASING**

Extreme Events

Wildfires	**MULTIPLYING**
Droughts	**INTENSIFYING**
Flash Floods	**DEVASTATING**
Hurricanes	**DESTRUCTIVE**
Storm Patterns	**UNPREDICTABLE**

This debt cannot be paid with currency. Accepting only immediate
environmental action and sustainable practices.

Chapter 1

THE PRICE WE NEVER MEANT TO PAY

Last winter, on a peaceful cold night, when city lights pierced the surrounding darkness, I stood with my father on the terrace. The day's noise softened into calm. At that time, I was discussing my higher studies. Suddenly I looked at him and asked, "Father, what did the night sky look like when you were little? Has the world changed a lot since then?"

He smiled, his gaze fixed on the stars. "How many can you see now?" he asked. I looked up and said, "Not many. I can count them."

He smiled again softly, but his words carried a hint of sorrow. "When I was a kid," he mentioned, "the night sky was magical. It wasn't just full of stars like a shining cover, like diamonds spread over a dark canvas. The atmosphere felt crisp, like rain mixed with soil." The air was fresh and cool, and sitting beneath those stars felt like a moment of peace.

He talked with a soft yearning, his voice filled with nostalgia. The ponds and lakes were clear and full of life. People could drink directly from them without filtration. The fields were lush and green, And the roads were lined with tall trees who offered shade like a parent beneath their branches. Mornings rang with the sweet songs of sparrows while winters brought graceful flocks of migratory birds, dancing across the sky. He waved his hand toward the scattered stars in the night sky, their weak light barely penetrating the darkness.

Instead of the melodious calls of birds, today's mornings greet the ear with the harsh noise of the alarm clocks. Ponds would now either be dried up or poisoned. Land covered in concrete has taken over fertile grounds, and trees have either disappeared or lain barren.

He stopped for some time, seemed that he was dewelling around the good memories from the past. He then continued the story; previously we have seen every season in its own unique way, they had the rhythms of nature's harmonic creation. Nowadays the seasons are unpredictable, warm and dry summer days now carry harmful heat waves and storms. In winter the sky used to be clear and known for the cool breeze but now it brings unexpected rains and storms. It is like, the nature's habits are fading day by day. I had seen a deep sadness in his voice.

I remembered all he said and it echoed in me like a gentle ache in my heart. I imagined a near future where we could never see a sky full of stars or breathe pure and fresh air. His memories were not merely a reflection of the past; they were quiet forewarnings of things we might lose.

I gathered my senses and looked around and found out that the beauty he was explaining was not extinct but on the way to it. Maybe the nature is waiting for the healing hands from us who actually care about it, or it wants to rest for some time for healing. We need to change. I can feel the planet whispering through the quiet darkness: "There's still hope." At that moment, I understood that it is high time to begin with small steps toward making our planet better.

I have huge respect for each and every person, government, company, organization, NGO who is working towards sustainability putting nature first. But we need to understand the whole story and we need a path.

The Price of Progress

The conversation with my father, forced me to know when we started ruining the environment. The revolution that changed the world in the way it functions is the Industrial Revolution which started in the late 18th century. And the changes my father's generation is witnessing were the final chapters of a story that had already started with the first coal-powered steam engines in England.

In numbers if we want to measure the destruction, then there is a metric called atmospheric CO2 levels. Academic research shows that the levels have increased approximately by 50%, from 280 to 420 parts per million starting from 1750 to the present day. Don't think it off like a statistic, this is the human industrial activity signature we have written in our atmosphere.

The industry which sparked the Industrial Revolution was the textile industry. This provides a clear example of this transformation. In Manchester, England which was once known as "Cottonopolis" here the rise of mechanized cotton mills gave humans the taste of prosperity which absolutely came at a devastating environmental cost. The River Mersey which flows through the heart of this industrial belt became one of Europe's most polluted rivers. By the 1850s the fish disappeared from that river and the water most of the time ran black with industrial waste.

And almost the same stories unfolded around the globe. In the USA the rise of steel manufacturing changed the landscape of Pittsburg, it was known as "Steel City", where the skies became so dark at noon that streetlights used to be on throughout the day. The city's transformation came at a severe cost of its three rivers, Allegheny, Monongahela, and Ohio, which became so polluted that the water would peel paint off surfaces it touched, and acid rain became a common occurrence.

Now another biggest source of mankind's evolution was the oil industry's revolution which also had a lot of environmental consequences. The first commercial oil well was drilled in Pennsylvania in 1859, which seemed like a miracle progress. But now we know that the effect of fossil fuel consumption throughout these many years has been devastating, nearly 1.5 trillion tonnes of CO_2 released into our atmosphere since the industrial revolution began, and it's still ongoing.

But these are not pretty isolated stories of individual industries gone wrong. They represent a fundamental flaw like how we have structured our entire economic system from that time. The true cost of progress wasn't calculated in the ledgers by these growing industries. The clean air, pure water and stable climate nature provided, we took them for granted, assuming these were infinite resources and the exploitation was easier than proper maintenance. This fundamental thought, we now know, was devastatingly wrong.

And not only that, modern business practices have accelerated these trends, the quarterly profits have fascinated and overshadowed the long term harm to environmental conditions. Not only that the Global supply chains were very efficient for these businesses but have multiplied the environmental impact of every product we create. A single smartphone's production journey touches dozens of countries, each step adding to our collective environmental footprint.

However, we learn that these problems are deeply interconnected. When my father spoke about that, the stars were disappearing from the night sky, he was witnessing, just one symptom of a much larger systemic crisis. These industrial processes played an important role in dimming the stars, warming our oceans, acidifying the rain and altering the molecular level of our atmosphere.

As the night grew deeper and few visible stars twinkled above us, I realized that the environmental crisis is not just about individual companies' poor choices, it is about the system, which we have built in a hurry and we have built without understanding the true costs of this. And every factory, every mine, every industrial process is part of this large web that is covering our beautiful earth.

The empowering forces of innovation and entrepreneurship have fueled the industrial revolution which are being redirected toward environmental solutions. From renewable technologies to circular economy initiatives, businesses are now realizing they have awakened a bit now, and they think that protecting our environment is our duty.

And this miracle of realization is most important, I think, and this is a legacy for our industrial journey. The companies of today and tomorrow have understood this fundamental truth: there is no sustainable profit on a depleted planet.

The cool night breeze carried the sorrow of the city I felt, which is constantly reminding us about our industrialized world. Tomorrow as the sun rises, thousands of chimneys will once again release the toxic burden into our atmosphere. And each emission joins an unfolding story which began with those first steam engines over two centuries ago. Like invisible footprints in the air, these emissions tell a story of progress and peril, a story that continues to unfold in every corner of our industrialized world. To understand this story, we must first learn to see these footprints, that shape our future, even when they remain invisible to our eyes…

Chapter 2

THE FOOTPRINTS WE CANNOT SEE

Last year, I went to Puri Beach in Bhubaneswar, and I was walking near the waves. My feet were engraving a temporary mark on the sand. But when the waves are advancing towards me the footprints created by me have disappeared, and the beach is once again clean and pristine. If our carbon footprints could disappear like this, our world would be much cleaner.

Every dawn, somewhere in Manhattan's steel and glass canyons, thousands of ACs come back to life, which is required for us humans to get a "climate-controlled productivity." In these huge monuments, where modern businesses are running, millions of computers will soon illuminate, and every working desk will silently add notes to the global harmony of energy consumption. A single floor in these modern offices uses as much electricity as an entire village consumes in many parts of the world.

Just three continents away, somewhere in Southeast Asia, the sun is about to set and the last rays are powering the massive solar panels recently installed atop of a textile factory. Inside, hundreds of sewing machines are trying to meet humans' fashion requirements. The solar panels indeed represent a green initiative above, but the factory's true carbon story lies in every rotating thread wheel, every steam press activated, and every shipment dispatched to distant shores. All these impacts go far beyond just the electricity bills.

Now, let us travel to the West where sprawling tech campuses of the Southeast and West countries have data centers that hum day and night. The cooling systems don't work like us for a paycheck; they work overtime against the tropical heat. Each search query, let's say your Sunday brunch basanti pulao recipe, each cloud upload, like your first bicycle as memory, each stand up meeting adds to the digital carbon footprint. Here a single data center consumes as much power as 50,000 homes. Yet without these humming units our modern global economy would grind to a halt.

As we know the carbon footprint is invisible so that means it can pop up anywhere. Somewhere in the vineyards of France's Bordeaux region, centuries old wineries' needs have been changed, now they need modern refrigeration systems and climate controlled cellars to maintain the perfect temperature for aging wine, the wine that one might savor even a century later. A single large winery's annual carbon footprint can equal that of hundreds of cars on the road.

Now if you cross the Mediterranean to Morocco's bustling automotive plants, you will be able to see robots and humans work in synchronized harmony. Not stopping there, these huge factories represent a new wave of manufacturing in Africa. And yes we still have majority vehicles running on petrol or diesel (electric vehicles are not fully green unless they are powered by renewable energy sources). So each car assembled not only holds the carbon cost of its creation, from the energy-intensive aluminum smelting to the final robot-applied coat of paint, but also bears its own future carbon footprint.

In South Asia's bustling metropolises, the rapid industrialization is clearly visible in its AQI. In most of the major cities, the AQI is above 300 during winter months, which creates a toxic haze that blankets the urban landscape. The perfect storm occurs when agricultural burning combines with vehicle exhaust, industrial emissions etc. Sacred rivers that once sustained civilizations now run with foam-mixed industrial effluents. The carbon footprint of these urban centers casts a long shadow, and with each passing day of industrial activity leaves an invisible but lasting mark on our atmosphere that will take decades of forest growth to absorb.

A carbon footprint, at the core level is a dark shadow that we are casting on our Earth's atmosphere. CO2e, Carbon dioxide equivalent is a concept, when we break it down it will seem less abstract: A single business flight between major south asian cities generates about 0.17 tons of CO2e which is equivalent to what an average tree absorbs over ten years of its lifetime.

The numbers are actually scary. Globally, businesses, industries alone contribute approximately 70% of the world's carbon emissions. In south asia alone, few sectors like commercial and industrial, account for nearly 60% of the region's electricity consumption. Each kilowatt-hour of electricity generated from coal, which remains the primary power source in many developing nations, releases approximately 0.82 kg of CO2 into the atmosphere.

When Small Actions Cast Long Shadows

Picture a little raindrop falling into a still big pond. Though it is little, the ripple it creates is not so little, we can see it affects a large area that is insignificant, not only that it joins countless other drops and creates waves that reach the shore. Our daily business activities which are absolutely essential casts similar ripples in our atmosphere, though we rarely see them.

In our busy lives we tend not to see these invisible footprints by different industries through a single day on our planet, let's trace them:

The blast furnaces at the steel mills roar at 1,700°C (3,092°F), which consumes enough energy in just one day which can power nearly 900,000 homes. 1.85 tons of CO2 is released into the atmosphere per ton of steel production. The smallest yet big thing even the water cooling systems in these mills consume more electricity than a small town.

On the other side the silent chemical plants convert raw materials into our daily use products. A single pharmaceutical manufacturing line is more thirsty than a magnesium carbonate block; it requires ultra pristine water. The purification systems consume 50% more energy than standard water distillation. The HVAC systems need to maintain exact sterile conditions which consume as much energy as 1,000 households.

The purification systems consume 50% more energy than standard water distillation. While exact numbers may vary, we can adopt a strategy of focusing on relative impact rather than absolute figures throughout the chapters.

Next, our food industry has its own carbon story. At 230°C (446°F) your favorite bread or croissant is baking in the industrial bakeries for hours. A single huge scale bakery's daily energy consumption equals that of 2,000 homes. To keep things fresh they have flash freezing units which draw power equivalent to running 500 air conditioners continuously.

Agricultural processing plants run without getting tired. The total energy consumed by a single grain drying facility in one season is equivalent to electricity needs for 4,000 houses throughout a year. Even the dairy industry uses 1,000 kilowatt-hours to process 100,000 liters of milk.

Yes we still have the majority of people read the print media, and in printing facilities, massive presses run 24/7. Only an hour of energy use by a contemporary printing machine matches the electricity needs of 40 average residential households. Printer systems dedicate 60% of their total energy consumption during paper drying operations alone.

The hospitality industry adds its own verses to this carbon symphony. A standard hotel room produces 31 kilograms of CO_2 daily. A medium-sized restaurant uses a quantity of power that exceeds the combined electricity needs of ten homes. A typical industrial laundry operation needs 3 gallons of 75°C (167°F) heated water to clean each weight of laundry.

Manufacturing tells an even bigger story; The average power consumption of an automotive assembly line robot exceeds 8 megawatt-hours during annual operation. Plastic injection molding machines consume 100 kilowatt-hours of power during each operating hour. One semiconductor fabrication plant requires enough daily water consumption to support all residents within a city of 40,000 people.

There is a deep footprint created by the beverage industry. Beer is one of the most common drinks around the world and the production of one barrel of that at a brewery consumes around 1,500 kilojoules of heat energy. Not only that, another most common, the soft drinks, The line where it gets ready for you to take a sip with your burger, requires a total of 300,000 kilowatt-hours monthly. Not only that the refrigeration systems used in beverage warehouse storage facilities use enough electricity to power 3,000 homes simultaneously.

Now the monster industry, the construction sites add their huge impact on carbon footprint. Approx 900 kg of CO2 is being produced per ton of cement made by a cement kiln. The biggest cranes aka Tower cranes consume about 135 kilowatt-hours per day. The Welding operations done in large projects use enough electricity to power 200 homes.

Even when we are enjoying watching a wonderful film, that entertainment industry also casts its shadow. A big film studio's daily power consumption is enough to power 2,000 residential homes. Our favorite concert venue cooling systems draw the same power as a small factory. Broadcasting equipment for a TV station consumes energy equivalent to 500 households.

The mining industry's energy appetite is more than any other industry till now. The large haul trucks with the tire diameter of ~70 inches burn 134 liters of diesel per hour. Rock crushing giants consume 150 kilowatt hours per ton of material. The deep mines also need water and their pump systems there use more electricity than small cities.

Why these numbers are important we may not consider them but these numbers just paint only part of the picture. Behind each statistic lies a cascade of supporting activities:

Maintenance operations consume their own energy share. Quality control systems running 24/7. Waste management processes require additional power, and 80% of around the world is not managed. Climate control systems working constantly. Safety and security systems never sleep.

Beyond the Bottom Line,
The Figures We Choose Not to See

Every morning, in corporate boardrooms around the world where directors, and executives gather to review colorful charts and graphs. The green arrow's upward direction creates smiles, on the other hand down arrow sparks questions. Success is measured in clean and crisp numbers like revenue growth, profit margins, market share, return on investment, CAGR, etc.

Now think about it, suddenly the screen of the computer or projector revealed a new column that clearly shows the actual cost of each business decision. Alongside the profit margins there is a new column labeled "Environmental Impact." And what if there is a new rule popped up the market share had to account for our share of nature's resources?

Our business scorecards are good at playing hide and seek with reality. We generally celebrate a factory or a manufacturing plant's record breaking production month, but the scorecard doesn't show the tons of microplastics released into nature. We celebrate when reduced production costs but the calculator ignores the ancient forests which have been cleared for raw materials.

For us ethics matters, but unknowingly we tend to forget that and rely upon cheap electrons generated by non-renewable sources. Many leading investment firms each year celebrate their "most efficient quarter", yes measured by old school metrics only. The algorithm they have used for trading executed millions of transactions per second using their power-hungry servers. But the quarterly report doesn't have that data which can show their data centers consume as much electricity as a small nation.

I will give you an example of the headlines of a successful annual report:

"Revenue up 40%!" shout the headlines.

"Profit margins expanded to 35%!" declare the analysts.

"Market capitalization doubled!" celebrate the investors.

But few metrics don't reach the powerpoint slide. There is a famous saying, "The things we can see we care about the most". I wonder if we can able to see electricity flowing like a river then we might have cared a bit. We are never able to see an honest report if we can then it might be like this:

"Water bodies tainted by textile dyes"

"Soil degraded by intensive cotton farming"

"Communities impacted by factory emissions"

"Species displaced by industrial expansion"

Basically the success metrics we follow are like a weighing scale that only measures in pounds or kgs, but ignores the stones crushing beneath its feet.

PART 2:
REIMAGINING BUSINESS

Chapter 3

NATURE'S BLUEPRINT

❧

The Masters of Sustainability

Nature is a creative artist. California contains the ancient redwood forests which feature tall ancient trees that reach sky-high heights. The location contains ancient trees which have survived for over two thousand years while observing multiple human evolutions and numerous civilizations that rose and fell. These trees are a great example of maintaining our earth's one of the most perfect sustainable systems. In a single acre of these old redwood forests, You will find more biomass than almost anywhere else on our earth. They store more carbon than any other ecosystem we know.

But the true magic is not that these mighties are touching the sky, it happens beneath our feet. These forests have created on their own what our modern economics struggle to achieve, a zero waste circular system where every output becomes an input. When these giants' needles fall, branches crash down, or even when a mighty trunk finally surrenders to time, nothing is wasted. Every microscopic substance or particle begins a new journey through a complex web of decomposition and renewal.

Studies and research have shown a single fallen redwood can take years to decompose, in this process also it contributes to the ecosystem. The decomposing wood becomes what ecologists termed a "nurse log," which hosts thousands of species of insects, fungi, microorganisms, etc. And as the natural system the log releases nutrients, where the next generation of trees will grow. The system is a perfect example of efficiency. You might find carbon atoms in a young redwood sapling today, that is cycling through the same forest as Roman Empire.

In the Indus Valley over 4500 years ago, there was an ancient civilization of Harappa and Mohenjo-daro. This civilization provides a remarkable example of sustainable urban planning. These cities have shown an extraordinary understanding of resource management and environmental harmony. The drainage systems they used to have were precisely engineered to prevent flooding and maintain sanitation. The Great Bath of Mohenjo-daro shows how they value and manage water resources, and they have careful water conservation systems. Their architectural designs incorporated natural ventilation and cooling systems, similar to modern passive cooling techniques. The cities' grid layout and advanced waste management systems reveal a civilization that understood the delicate balance between urban development and environmental sustainability.

Now yes we need to admire those thoughts which are made upon nature's principles. The famous architecture, the Eastgate Centre in Harare, Zimbabwe, a 333,000 square foot shopping center and office complex uses 0 modern HVAC systems, but still maintains a comfortable temperature throughout the year. The magic here is the design is inspired by the termites of the African savanna, they also known as "The self cooling macrotermes michaelseni"

These termites maintain a perfect temperature of 30.5°C in their habitation, despite any temperature outside. For years the architects have studied this natural model and discovered how tiny insects created natural ventilation using the physics of convection currents. This architectural genius uses 90% less energy than a conventional building with the same size.

Now let's go to the gigantic water bodies and the vast oceans, where whales have understood their own form of amazing design. According to conventional fluid dynamics the humpback whale can not execute very close turns, but they nailed in that. Now where is the magic here, it is in their flippers, which are hidden in bumps called tubercles. Scientists say these irregular bumps create required vortices in the water, resulting in reduced drag and increased lift. Now again understanding this and applying it to follow nature's high level design principle is smart and great work. WhalePower Corporation applied this design to the industrial fans and wind turbines, they achieved significant energy efficiency improvements.

Now another magic of nature, the lotus leaf. One of the important aspects of sustainability is self maintenance. I have seen this magic because lotus is common in Asia's ponds and lakes. In the muddy waters they look pristine and clean. Now the surface of the leaves is covered with many tiny bumps which are also coated with natural wax. Humans have learned/inspired by this natural design principle and created self cleaning paints, fabrics, solar panels etc, it also expands the lifespan.

Now how can we forget the master of magic by nature? Every leaf in this world is a solar kitchen, which operates on quantum efficiency levels, the photosynthetic process. This is still our dream to create solar panels to match the same efficiency. The light harvesting complex in plants achieves nearly 100% quantum efficiency, converting every photon to electrons in ideal conditions. To compare with the efficiency we have achieved is ~40%. Nature's solar technology not only captures energy but it simultaneously confiscates carbon and produces oxygen and also creates food. For us humans, nearly every calorie we consume is directly or indirectly from the sun and plants; yes this is a fundamental fact we first learned in elementary school.

Now there are many biomimicry like this, we will talk more about this. But why? because these are not only examples of magic or just solve one's curiosities. They show the longest running R&D on Earth. Nature has been perfecting sustainable solutions for billions of years, not as isolated experiments but as interconnected components of a vast, complex system. Every solution developed goes through an ultimate test of long term sustainability within the limits of our Earth's resources. The best we can do is use the already tried and tested models in different environments by nature, understand them and build on that same sustainable principle.

Now as per our current environmental conditions we are not in a good state. These natural innovations are more than an inspiration. They provide the blueprint, but that path with the luxury we want is hard to follow so that's why we fall for cheap and easy solutions. Now I don't think anyone thinks that nature's solution doesn't work. The main question in our context is: how we can transform or create our business practices which will align with these time tested nature's principles?

Learning from Nature's Business Models

Last year, I was reading about the Coral Reef, and watched a documentary about the Great Barrier Reef. A vibrant coral reef is a living network, home to thousands of organisms from tiny coral polyps (anemones) to majestic parrotfish, which plays a significant role. There is no single king or someone who is getting only benefited from that ecosystem, it is an interdependent community. The underwater is still a mystery to us. In this coral city waste is converted into nourishment, and competition seems like collaboration.

These dynamic ecosystems gave us profound lessons which allowed us to rethink our business practices.

In today's industrial landscape, we being isolated entities, are in pursuit of short-term gains. But what if businesses work like coral reefs, where success of each of the sapiens being is counted and supports the entire mankind? Maybe it is happening somewhere in the world, on a very small scale but we can envision an "eco network" where each of the businesses share resources in a decentralized, regenerative system where waste from one model or process becomes the raw material for another. A model where energy, water, and all other materials flow in continuous cycles, gives room to nature's ability to renew them endlessly.

Same if we look for land we will find millions of forest canopies around the world. We can reimagine the concept of industrial symbiosis through the lens of these canopies. In a natural forest each fallen leaf enriches the soil, they think about the future of the new generation.

If we think about a tree it is nature's perfect business model. It creates its own energy, recycles all its waste not only that it provides free shelter for the end no of species. It gives nature the precious things but won't stop growing every year it grows more substantial. For a tree it measures success not its quarterly profit but in rings by which humans can calculate the tree's contribution to nature from a sapling. What if businesses learned to count their growth rings in the same way?

Nature has the most sustainable business models, but we often overlook them because we don't spend time building on top of that or the artificial alternatives are too easy to work with on. Like for example in India, our ancient temples and monuments which maintain a comfortable temperature without any need of modern air conditioning. If we go to village areas the traditional houses made with clay stay cool in summer and warm in winter. The true finding is these structures work in harmony with the natural principles rather than against them. But today we are racing towards easy and artificial solutions while destroying the natural principles. The irony is hard but true not everyone will like it but - even as we search for water and life on Mars, we continue to deplete Earth's resources. The path forward is clear if we think properly: we need to integrate natural resources into our business models in a way that respects their processes and limitations. And what we're taking from nature, we need to equally give back to nature to balance it. This isn't just environmental stewardship - it's smart business.

I remember once I visited Haldia there I went to the coastal area where fishing communities stay. During normal conversation, there was one old person who told me "fishing was their primary profession once" He also told me twenty years ago we celebrated by seeing how full our nets were. but today we are happy thinking how many fish we leave in the sea". They had learned the hard truth: profit without preservation is like eating the seeds of next year's harvest.

What if we translate this principle into a business model where companies trade physical byproducts along with knowledge base, innovations while maintaining a healthy competitiveness, which can actually convert liabilities into assets. Like picture a cluster of enterprises where a technology firm repurposes the high temperature waste from a manufacturing plant to power their data centers. And also the same plant utilizes organic waste to generate bioenergy. Now here the two p's (profit and planet) complement each other, and work in harmony.

Now we can think about the idea of "evolutionary business," a model based on the genius process of natural selection. Just as species, including humans, have evolved through trial, error, and adaptation, companies can create business ecosystems that are both agile and self-correcting. In the process of building we can learn from each market shift as forests adapt themselves through seasonal rains, continuously learning and evolving their way of survival and growth. This is not an immediate profit margin kind of thing, it requires long term thinking, follow the path of resilience and constant learning.

Okay another one, the field regenerative finance, where nature's resource cycles inspire another dimension in the economy. Let's say there are global metrics of measuring the regenerative impact each business creates. The success is not measured only by financial returns but actually by investing in the health of their local ecosystems, like a natural wetland which stores water but purifies the air over decades. Small and meaningful steady changes by each company can create a big change and restore a lot.

Nature's principles are based on honesty and transparency. In our current digital world as blockchain tech is increasing we can develop decentralized processes where each node can validate the authenticity of transactions, resources shared, and origin of a product just like the processes followed by nature's mycorrhizal network. I am not talking about a regular technical upgrade; it will be a fundamental pivot towards systems where transparency, mutual support matters.

We can think about these transformative models which can be implemented with deep, thoughtful research and learning. We don't need to focus on whether these methods will work in a boardroom or not, we need to focus on how quickly we can learn and fix our models because when it will be too late we can't revert back. There is no one powerful in front of nature, if it wants and we cross our limits it will take a few seconds to wipe out the whole mankind from history.

Showcasing Pioneers on Nature's Frontier

Now it is not that companies around the world are not evolving, they are evolving around the globe. The conventional business landscape is changing, by taking inspiration directly from nature. I will take a few examples around the world who care about nature. The stories are as diverse as the ecosystems. These pioneers are proving to us that sustainability and profitability can coexist, most importantly they are showing us a blueprint for how business can respect and rejuvenate the natural environment.

Let's travel around the world and see what is changing.

In the USA, the sports gear giant Adidas made a groundbreaking partnership with Parley for the oceans, the first source of life on our planet. Together, they have transformed ocean plastic waste, a consequence of human irresponsibility, into high-performance athletic gear. Every product they have crafted with those plastic waste shows us a radical shift. Yes we are facing a worldwide pollution crisis, turning that into a resource with innovation is excellent. This is nature's way of giving us a second chance. When you run in these shoes you will join the movement that honors nature's capacity to heal itself.

Now almost half a world away in the forests of Sweden, IKEA is reimagining the future of home furnishing through a circular economic model. Their lab is that circular lab where discarded household items and damaged furniture get a new life into new designs. 97.8% of the wood used for IKEA is from Forest Stewardship Council® certified (FSC®) or recycled. Did you find the similarity with our nature? They are much like the forest floor that recycles its organic matter. It started as a hopeful idea but now writing industry benchmarks. Their products blend design, sustainability and consumer experience into one story.

Now if we travel to India, We will see along with many other companies, ITC and Godrej have woven sustainability into their core fabric. They have invested heavily in renewable energy, water conservation and reforestation initiatives. Godrej's commitment shows how we humans can build eco-friendly products, also align with sustainable practices. Their projects are inspired by nature's own process of renewal. All these initiatives benefit the bottom line and affect the lives of thousands positively.

If we move to a bit north in India, Phool has created a unique story of circular economy. They are addressing two big environmental challenges together. One, they collect around 21 tonnes of temple flowers per week, which would anyways go in waste or pollute rivers, and Second they create natural incense sticks and other sustainable products out of that. Their 'flowercycling' model prevents pollution and also provides employment to a lot of people. They have an innovative green leather named as 'Fleather' which is also made from floral waste, won the PETA Innovation Award. Phool's example clearly shows how traditional practices with modern innovation can create sustainable businesses that will benefit both the environment and the society.

Now Europe, You must have heard about Unilever and Acciona, who also followed nature's blueprint with remarkable results. Unilever's sustainable living brands reengineer every ingredient, process and packaging which minimize the environmental impact. Their initiatives also echo the natural world where each and every smallest component like a pollinator to sprawling forests plays a critical role which forms a perfect balance. Acciona, on the other hand, is pioneering renewable energy sources and sustainable construction, utilizing every available renewable energy source from nature to provide innovative sustainable solutions. They perfectly mirror the natural cycle of energy use and consumption. But their operations are limited to those places, we need to see, learn and implement the big picture.

Over in Germany Siemens and BMW show a commitment to perfect resource management. Siemens is one of the leaders in the smart grid technology, their portfolio includes energy distribution automation, smart metering, etc which we can termed as "self regulating circular economy." On the other hand BMW has pushed their way forward in the electric mobility segment, all the models that start with "i" are all electric in their portfolio. They take recycling of material very seriously on the same principle based on nature's three fold cycle renewal, reuse and regeneration.

Emerging markets like China and Russia, where the industrial revolution has played an important role, are also in this new wave of forward thinking. According to reports in 2019 China was responsible for 28% of global CO2 emissions. China aims to source 80% of its total energy consumption from renewable sources by 2060. Russia is also too aggressive with their thoughts on natural resilience.

There are numerous companies actively pursuing sustainability. Each case represents a significant step in this collective movement. For innovation and a generation-long change we need to dare to think like that. In doing so, these companies reaffirm a profound truth which is that when we build with nature rather than against it, we create systems that are not only more sustainable but also inherently more resilient and beautiful.

The Profitable Path of Stewardship

As we are progressing through the chapters it is getting clear that environmental stewardship is not just an ethical choice but it is becoming an economic imperative. We don't need to choose between profit and planet anymore, the two are inextricably linked.

Just imagine this: When a company reduces its energy consumption with the help of renewable sources it cuts the carbon emissions. When the company thinks about circularity and puts that concept to build a product, on one hand it is preserving the resources and along with that generates multiple revenue streams with the concept of recycling and refurbishment.

I recently analyzed a few reports of the companies who have embraced environmental stewardship. I can see the patterns clearly. The companies which have invested in renewable energy sources are now understanding the benefits of reduced operational costs. Around the globe solar panel prices have dropped by more than 80% in the past 10 years.

And not only that we can see the shift in consumer behavior, modern customers are now aware of the benefits of sustainability so they are willing to pay more for the sustainable products.

The path forward for us is very clear, environmental stewardship is a catalyst in the path of profitability.

Chapter 4

THE GREEN REVOLUTION IN THE BOARDROOM

☙❧

The Anatomy of Organizational Transformation

Everytime we think about it, a boardroom where the air is thick with the weight of the decisions made. The oak wood table is polished, the ergonomic chairs are arranged with minute precision, a smart screen is illuminated with charts and graphs having millions of numbers. But is not something missing? Yes as we discussed in the previous chapters the metrics of success the cost to the planet data are missing. Organizational transformation is not like installing solar panels on the roof or changing all the lights to LED, yes these matter but it is not the change I am talking about.

The heart of true organizational transformation comes from the Triple Bottom Line framework: People, Planet and Profit. This concept is from John Elkington, which changes the way we measure business success fundamentally. This approach demands equal attention to social equity (People), environmental impact (Planet), and economic value (Profit). These are like filters of any business decision. For example if there is a new manufacturing process is coming up it should be evaluated on not just its cost efficiency but also its environmental footprint and the impact it creates on the people involved into it. The core idea is to understand the long term business success is impossible without taking care of social and environmental sustainability. The Triple Bottom Line should be a compass to navigate through the complex landscape of a modern business.

In many organizations, sustainability is like an afterthought of a huge decision. Yes, it is in the system and running from the past. Sometimes it is a tick box, or a slogan to print on annual reports. There is an invisible wall, a barrier which separates environmental ethics from the core of business operations. And this wall is what keeps sustainability in the periphery, far from the heart which makes the decisions.

Yes it is technical but neurological too. the invisible wall needs to break.

And the main change should start with the leadership, if they want the whole system to work differently they can. It should not be enough for a CEO to give just a speech about sustainability once a year. The entire leadership team, the board of directors, CEO, CTO, COO whoever is there in that decision making chair must align, commit and will to rethink the way their company should operate. This is strictly not like appointing a sustainability officer or launching a green initiative.

And it is not an overnight thing, what current big successful companies are doing, is also correct. Like they are creating a parallel green structure for these green transitions. In this approach there is always a room for experimentation without risking the core operations. Slowly but consistently we need to embed sustainability into every aspect of the business from product design to supply chains, from employee engagement to customer communication.

The first thing is, if it is a product based company we need to measure the total carbon emissions per unit starting from raw material extraction until the product reaches the customer. We should also write that info in the label to educate the customers, and let them know how inherently carbon footprint is present in us. As Business Management Expert, Peter Drucker says "You Can't Manage What You Can't Measure" so let's start measuring, it may need a team of R&D that will research about the actual data, but it is worth it.

Then how we are sourcing the raw material, considering whether they come from sustainable suppliers or certified sources that meet regulatory standards. Equally important is evaluating how we generate the energy to run our operations, particularly whether we rely on fossil fuels or renewable sources. Then comes how efficiently the resources are being used like the water, energy, raw material, etc. Sustainability should not be a cost center but it should be a value driver.

But only leadership is not enough to change into a green boardroom. Like everyone in the ecosystem brings something, same as every employee, even customers should feel empowered to contribute to this process. This means just training programs or colored recycling bins are not enough. We need to create a new culture where sustainability is a part of daily conversations.

Now comes to the critical part in boardrooms and huge offices where HVAC systems are running on overtime. Traditional systems drink more energy and contribute heavily to the operational carbon footprints. We can shift to green HVAC solutions but what would be better is geothermal heating and cooling systems. Earth's stable underground temperature works like magic. We can change the existing buildings' design to incorporate this or convert them to work like that by using innovation and modern technology. Also IOTs need to be packed with AI which will in real time check the occupancy of the floor or machines being used or the current weather to strain out only the energy that is needed.

Zero waste, it seems easy but not so. Every corporate office, company should operate on a zero waste model, not even paper cups. We can start auditing waste and can understand where it is coming from, major sources can be identified with this. The best will be switching to reusable but hygienic options or suppliers who actually will take back the biodegradable waste and then recycle them accordingly.

There can be multiple solutions regarding sustainability in every sector, every business, we need to think about it; if an MNC or startup can crack a complex data algorithm, this thinking will be nothing for them. We need to constantly monitor the sustainability reports for each month and understand where it is lacking. This holistic approach will guide others, and the system will be forced to make mandatory compliances regarding green shifts.

The Transformative Journey: Stories of Change

The first story comes from Denmark's industrial region. The company is Ørsted formerly known as DONG Energy, the company is also known for Europe's most coal intensive company. According to the records, in 2008 Dong Energy was responsible for one third of Denmark's whole carbon emissions. Their transformation journey began with a grand announcement but strategic realization. The business model was unsustainable both environmentally and economically.

They went through multiple strategic shifts and were also supported by the Danish government, and they were shown one of the most remarkable green transitions in corporate history. After over a decade of slow transitions, Ørsted reduced its carbon emissions by 86%. They have rethought their entire business model. Today, Ørsted has become a global leader in offshore wind power. And this black-to-green journey is not just about changing technologies, It is about changing mindsets, retraining workers, and rebuilding an entire corporate culture around sustainability.

In Japan, there was another story brewing, a different kind of transformation was taking place. Ricoh, the printing and imaging company, has faced challenges that are common to many manufacturing companies. What they came up with is the concept of "Comet Circle," their approach to a circular economy. They began designing products with the end of life in mind; they have introduced a comprehensive take-back program that aimed to recycle and reuse a maximum amount of their product range. One of their products, the printers, can now easily be disassembled, and the parts can be reused or recycled. They have even developed special screws that are easy to remove in the recycling process. Small details can speak volumes about the company's commitment to sustainability.

Now this is the story of Interface, a global carpet manufacturer, which shows another perspective on transformation. In 1994, the founder, Ray Anderson, got a "spear in the chest" moment after reading "The Ecology of Commerce" by Paul Hawken. A company which was heavily dependent on petroleum based products and also generating a significant waste, the path to a sustainable model was seem impossible. But Interface launched "Mission Zero" in 1994, they took a commitment which is still going on and by 2040 they are aiming to be a carbon negative company. Their principle for this is AVOID, REDUCE, STORE, INSPIRE. They have invented a new manufacturing process for the carpets, created them such a way they can be recycled endlessly, and also developed ways to capture and reuse carbon.

There is one small company, Dutch chocolate maker Tony's Chocolonely, whose story is very inspiring. Their operations are not only green, they have changed the entire industry's approach to sustainability. The entire business model is built around social and environmental responsibility. They had a mission to eliminate slavery from the chocolate industry and they have achieved that by creating a transparent supply chain which ensures cocoa farmers receive fair wages through their '5 Sourcing Principles'. Not only that their farming practices are sustainable, and by seeing their success the large manufacturers followed that suit.

Now let's talk about a giant, Google, who has billions of users, and their data centers consume a vast amount of energy. In 2007 they made a commitment to be carbon neutral by 2012, they have achieved this by 2017. And from nearly two decades google has signed more than 115 agreements which sums up to 14 GW of clean energy. Along with that Google's

Deepmind AI it can analyze patterns of power consumption which reduced the data center cooling costs by 40%. Now Google's next goal is to achieve 24/7 Carbon-Free Energy by 2030.

Now, it is a totally different story, but with the same narrative. In the construction industry, LafargeHolcim faced a unique challenge. The total CO2 emissions from cement manufacturing represent approximately 8% of worldwide. Holcim projects its carbon footprint reductions at maximum levels between 2030 and 2050 and the Science Based Targets initiative (SBTi) has approved these targets. They have redefined their products, they have created ECOPlanet, a new line of low-carbon cement, which uses alternative materials like calcined clay and recycled construction waste. Not only this, The company has invested in technology known as CCUS (carbon capture, utilization, and storage) which enables the capture of CO2 emissions before their entry into the atmosphere.

There are thousands of stories like this. These stories have a common thread: they are awakened to the bad things happening to the nature. None of these transformations were easy or quick, over night thing. They required vision, commitment, and sometimes significant investment. Also these transitions are not just adding a layer of sustainability to their business, they have changed the idea fundamentally. They have also shown us that the path to a sustainable future is not just possible, it is profitable too.

The Leadership Blueprint for Sustainable Change

Leadership directly affects the whole company. When it comes to corporate sustainability there are many million dollar companies are creating stories. I will take the example of two huge companies.

Apple, the company is a trend setter and it is setting trends in terms of sustainability also. Apple has made its 2030 sustainability commitments pretty clear. The leadership team has structured the whole plan in a way that it covers business operations, manufacturing, supply chain, the whole product life cycle, etc. Their report says in 2023 22% of materials shipped in the products are from recycled and renewable sources. In the supply chain part Apple partnered with 320 suppliers who committed to use 100% renewable electricity by 2030. Apple also says that its entire product portfolio will become carbon neutral by 2030. They have identified the three biggest sources of greenhouse gas emissions, the electricity, materials and transportation and rigorously working on that motto. The results are also clear: there has been a 55% reduction in CO_2 emissions since 2015. They have a recycling robot Daisy, which can disassemble 200 devices per hour. The company's journey shows that, how strategic planning can bring a huge sustainable change.

Now if you are looking for a textbook example of across-the-board environmental stewardship example then Microsofts story can help. They also created industry responsibility standards through their environmental commitments and first announcement in 2020. Their leadership team has a clear four pillar strategy which revolves around becoming carbon negative by 2030, becoming water positive, achieving zero waste and protecting more land than they use. Not only this their report says they will remove all of the company's emitted carbon since its founding in 1975 by 2050. We can see the results prominently. In FY23, Microsoft invested in 23.6 million MWh of renewable energy (enough to power Paris for two years), diverted 18,537 metric tons of waste from landfills, contracted 61.7 million cubic meters of water replenishment benefits, and protected 15,849 acres of land (exceeding their target by 40%).

These companies are showing that technology companies should think towards sustainable leadership which will eventually build a future of green tomorrow.

The Power of People: Employee Engagement in the Green Revolution

Employees play a significant role in aligning the dots set by the leadership team. Like the same happened to Lush Cosmetics. Lush encourages their employees by involving them directly in its ethical campaigns and product creation processes. This includes developing products with minimal packaging. This creates a healthy culture of innovation and the innovation stays with the company's core values and integrates sustainability into the employees.

Another major company is Starbucks. They have implemented a sustainability program for all the employees, also known as "partners", which educates them about companies sustainability goals. These learning includes waste reduction, ethical sourcing, and energy efficiency. Not only that, Starbucks also encourages their partner to lead local community service projects which are related to environmental stewardship. These grassroots approaches actually create the change we want to see.

One of the most creative companies is Adobe. Their approach is more gamified. They have a team called "Green Team" where all team members are a volunteer group. They work on projects to reduce the company's environmental impact. The team leads many small but important initiatives like waste reduction, recycling, and promoting sustainable commuting options. Adobe supports these kinds of efforts by providing proper resources and recognition.

And as always, there are more stories; these stories show us that when employees are genuinely engaged and empowered, they can accelerate the pace in achieving the company's sustainability goals. We just need to give them the proper tools and opportunities so that they can contribute.

Chapter 5

TOMORROW'S TOOLS TODAY

The Urban Renaissance

Businesses are a huge part of our society. I have started writing this book focusing only on the business part of it but I think I need to talk about this because we can replicate this in the business world directly or take inspiration from this.

In the heart of Copenhagen, a green revolution in urban living is quietly showing up. The morning sun glimmers on the angular slopes of CopenHill (Amager Bakke), the world's most innovative power plant. It is a waste to energy power plant, an architectural marvel which generates clean energy by incinerating waste and supplies electricity to tens of thousands of homes in Copenhagen. It is like a playground of innovation on the basis of the idea of "hedonistic sustainability."

Copenhagen, the city's commitment to sustainable transport tells another compelling story. Nearly half of all the trips to work or school in Copenhagen happen on two wheels. They have over 400 km of dedicated bike lanes, these paths prioritized even in winter snowfall. The result is visible a 33% reduction in carbon emissions from transport compared to 2005 levels, with a goal of 50-60% by 2025.

Now let's fly to Singapore to witness the perfect harmony of nature and architecture. The Supertree Grove at Gardens by the Bay consists of 18 vertical gardens, each structure reaching heights of 25 to 50 meters, all looking like a forest of mechanical marvels. And they are not just for show, they host 162,900 plants from around 200 species, one of the world's most iconic green infrastructure projects. When the sun is up they harvest solar energy and then at night they illuminate with that energy which proves that sustainable infrastructure can be both functional and breathtaking.

Ljubljana, Slovenia's green capital, shows us like an ecosystem, how even the smallest creatures can play a crucial role in urban sustainability. The city's "bee path" initiative makes them a leader in urban beekeeping. This led to 4500 beehives. These pollinators not only produce honey but also contribute to biodiversity in green urban spaces. Their city center is car free and the line between urban development and nature blurs, which is a live lab of sustainable city.

Amsterdam is pretty strict with plastics. Their waterways showcase another dimension of urban innovation. The city's bubble barrier technology, where a stream of bubbles rises from the canal bed which then captures the plastic waste before it enters into the ocean. This is a very simple but effective solution which often combines with community-led "plastic fishing" initiatives. Together, these efforts keep the city's canals clean while redirecting collected plastics for recycling, demonstrating how circular economy principles can transform urban waste management.

Each city has created its own unique path to adopt sustainability, proving that there's no one size fits all solution to urban environmentalism. It is all about making spaces where communities can live happily, where innovation meets tradition, and where every citizen plays a part in developing a better tomorrow.

The Symphony of Innovation

In a sleek lab in Switzerland, a window is doing extraordinary things. The window is not just keeping the cold out, it is generating electricity. These transparent solar cells are developed by École Polytechnique Fédérale de Lausanne (EPFL) that can generate electricity while also allowing visible light to pass through. They capture invisible wavelengths of the sunlight. And it is so capable that a single square meter can generate up to 50W of energy that can charge two smartphones daily. Now think about a skyscraper with these windows, it will be literally a "power house."

The oceans, too, are witnessing a bit of a quiet transformation. The world's most powerful tidal turbine, Orbital O2, spins beneath the waves of Scotland's Orkney Islands. It is like an underwater windmill, which harnesses the predictable power of the ocean currents. It generates about 2 MW, which is enough to power 2000 homes. The wind can be intermittent but the tidal energy follows the moon's reliable rhythm, which is almost constant.

Now in Norway's fjords, the world's first electric ferry glides silently in the water. The ferries are powered by this country's abundant hydroelectric power. Results are also visible, the carbon emissions have been reduced by 95% compared to diesel ferries. The operating costs of these are also very less. It is a live example of how maritime transport is also evolving, a perfect story that even traditional industries can also change.

Deep beneath Stockholm's streets, there is a unique partnership going on between the data centers and district heating systems. They have successfully implemented a heat recovery system where the excess heat from servers, once wasted, is now used to heat thousands of homes. A perfect example of circular thinking, one system's waste becomes another's resource, just like the redwood jungle. The Scandinavian city has converted its digital infrastructure into a source of warmth, it shows smart urban planning can find sustainable approaches in unexpected places.

Japan's Fukushima prefecture, once known for nuclear disaster, now is one of the world's largest green hydrogen production plants. It uses solar energy to generate hydrogen through electrolysis. The Fukushima Hydrogen Energy Research Field (FH2R) produces enough hydrogen to fuel 560 fuel cell vehicles daily, all it needs is sunlight and water. It is an example of how regions can reinvent themselves through clean technology.

These innovations are not a closed lab breakthrough, they are open, live and interconnected solutions which forms a new technological ecosystem. And also there is no set approach to go with a particular innovation, according to the situation the innovation evolves, the same as nature's rules, like region specific species or animals they have some capabilities to handle that particular environment. We should not wait for a single revolutionary technology to save us.

The First-Mover's Edge

When traditional battery manufacturers were hesitating ,a startup ,Northvolt Ett boldly built Europe's greenest battery factory powered primarily by hydroelectric and renewable energy .Despite a lot of issues and shortfalls they have secured over 55 billion in contracts from major automakers like Volkswagen ,Volvo ,BMW ,etc .Their early commitment to sustainable manufacturing has made them an industry leader from an unknown player.

Xylem, a water technology company, at a very early time understood that the water scarcity would become a global crisis. When others found out water management as more on the utility section, they provided smart water management solutions to address the water crisis. Today these solutions help utilities save billions of gallons of water. Their revenue reached $8.6 billion in 2024, which is a 16% increase from the previous year.

Now Ball Corporation's early pivot in the packaging industry, one of the largest industries, shows that there is another dimension where businesses can think. They have started long before the anti plastic movement has started. They are now a leader in infinitely recyclable aluminum packaging. This foresight has led them to partnerships with beverage giants worldwide. Their revenue grew by 12% in 2022 alone.

In Japan, Daikin industries have realized the future of cooling systems before others. They are a global leader in energy-efficient heat pumps and low-global-warming-potential (GWP) refrigerants. Their R-32 refrigerant has one third of the GWP traditional refrigerants have. Daikin's early innovation and understanding has definitely given them some edge in the world market of sustainable cooling solutions.

Brambles Limited, has shown another dimension, how early sustainability adoption changes the whole supply chain. Their business model is all about sharing and reusing pallets and containers. Brambles' CHEP platform prevents millions of tons of CO2 emissions annually while delivering superior shareholder returns.

Stora Enso's transformation from a traditional paper manufacturer to a renewable materials company shows a powerful lesson. They think and develop wood based alternatives to the fossil based materials. As every brand is looking for a sustainable change in packaging, their bio based materials complete those demands. Stora Enso also prioritizes sustainable forestry management practices to ensure the responsible sourcing of raw materials.

Tomorrow's tools today are not just about having an innovative technology, it is about having the courage to lead that as industry first. As markets evolve and environmental pressures mount, the question isn't whether to adopt sustainable practices, but when. And these stories show us, repeatedly, that those who move first don't just participate in the market transformation, they lead it.

PART 3: THE GREEN EPILOGUE

Chapter 6

BREAKING THROUGH THE BARRIERS

⚘

Understanding Resistance

Picture a mighty oak tree, whose roots are deeply entrenched in the soil, which is standing unmoved against the heavy winds of change. Actually like this oak tree our minds and organizations have grown very comfortably in established ways, creating invisible yet powerful barriers to transformation. These barriers are not made of concrete or steel, but of something far more formidable: human nature itself.

Our brains, and all other organs that are in us help us survive, sometimes ironically come in between our very changes for survival. The same way we also think when faced with the prospect of transforming business practices for environmental sustainability, our mental defense kicks in with precision of an ancient survival system. "We have always done it this way" becomes more than just a statement. It is more likely a shield we wrap ourselves in when confronted with change.

The Psychology of Resistance

I think that the resistance is stronger in three layers, each of them is more subtle than the previous one. The first is our psychological barrier, a recoil mechanism of our brain from change. Just like a person stepping back before going bungee jumping. It is an instinct which retreats from any major transformations, even when one knows that one is equipped with all the safety measures before jumping. In many boardrooms across the globe still hesitate to implement significant changes to the company because of not ignorance but the psychology of Resistance, it is one of the reasons, the brain's hardwired preference for the familiar over unknown.

The psychological resistance sometimes manifests as fear, fear of failure, fear of loss, fear of criticism, fear of the unknown. When a company considers switching or starting with renewable energy sources or implementing any cyclic principle of sustainability, the mind first thinks about the worst case scenarios, what if it costs too much? what if it disrupts an operation, what if it slows us down? What if the competitors gain an advantage? etc. these fears are natural but can paralyze the decision making and innovation of green change.

The weight of cognitive biases adds another layer of complexity. Status quo bias makes us overvalue current practices while also undervaluing potential improvements. Confirmation bias leads us to seek information that supports our existing beliefs about traditional business methods while dismissing evidence that supports sustainable alternatives. To break free from these mental shackles requires conscious effort and awareness.

The Organizational Fortress

The second layer is more deep, The organization interia. Think of it like this: a massive ship at sea is sailing towards shore, now changing its direction requires not only turning the wheel, but needing to overcome the momentum of thousands of tons of steel pushing forward in the actual original direction. Years of established practices, ingrained procedures, interconnected systems create the same momentum which resists any attempt of change.

The organizational inertia manifests in many different ways. The existing physical or digital infrastructure is a first call to change but that often seems too expensive or complicated to replace. The outdated legacy systems, still are running critical expensive operations. Think of a 10 year experienced professional employee who has carefully developed the skills over years are now often threatened by new AI changes happening around the global industries. For the case of AI we need to embrace that change, we can't stop that, same is for the sustainable changes in an organization. Even the organizational hierarchy that we still have can become a barrier. All these barriers are like filters where a change is diluted or delayed.

These challenges extend beyond regular systems and structures. The organizational culture that we are busy building for years, sometimes that invisible force is involved in shaping behavior and decision making. They can be the most formidable barrier of all. When these meaningful sustainability initiatives clash with deeply rooted cultural values or set established ways of working, the resistance can be fierce than anything. All these will lead to showing up not in outright rejection, but in subtle foot-dragging and lack of enthusiasm.

The Time Horizon Dilemma

The third and the most important layer is the most insidious barrier is our relationship with time. I am explaining how humans evolved from thousands of years to respond to immediate threats, even though that is nature's rule. Like you are camping in the woods, and the rustling you see might be a predator, the dark clouds show us it can be an approaching heavy storm. But climate change, environmental degradation operate in a different timescale in our mind, until and unless it is too late or damaged. Basically they are like slow rising tide not like a crashing wave. And we postpone slow things and prefer short term gains.

And this short term versus long term thinking creates friction, we know that we need to act. In our day to day life, even small things we know switching off light for even 1 hour can sum up to a large number at the end of the year. But the urgency to act gets diluted in the vast ocean of daily priorities and quarterly targets. The pressure to deliver immediate results, deadlines overshadows the need for long term sustainability investments. The gravitational pull of short term thinking is very tempting.

The quarterly reporting cycle of companies intensifies this challenge. The executives, decision makers find themselves torn between implementing necessary long term green initiatives and daily standup expectations. This temporal tension creates a form of organizational schizophrenia. Think of it like this, we know what we need to do for sure for a better future but still we are held accountable for immediate results.

Breaking Through

These barriers weaved and reinforced each other in the system, a web that can trap the most well structured sustainability initiatives. Understanding them is not about assigning blame or something like that, It is about recognizing them, addressing them, they are as natural as gravity. Like early aviators who first had to understand gravity before they could defy it, we must first comprehend these resistances before we can transcend them.

We can start with the smallest unit of change, from the mind. "Green rooms" a concept which is already there, basically dedicated spaces where teams can experiment with sustainable changes without fear of failure. When a manufacturing team tests a new recycling process or a product design group explores more eco-friendly material, they are not just solving problems, they are building confidence in change itself.

Now for the time horizon gap we need to bridge a few transform metrics. What if along with quarterly targets, there are metrics named as "horizon metrics" which track progress across different time periods. Okay picture this, a dashboard where immediate wins like (x amount of energy saved this month), medium term progress (carbon reduction in this year), and long term impact (planned environmental benefit goals achieved over 5 years). When a logistics company tracks both fuel costs saved today and projected emissions reduced over years, it creates a narrative of progress that satisfies both immediate and future needs.

Now we can build "change champions" networks across every hierarchy of the organization. They are not just sustainability officers, they are actual in-field or assigned project workers or employees, who discover a way to reduce waste, the accountant who develops new ways to measure environmental impact, the sales representative who helps clients understand the value of green products. Give these champions both authority and resources. When they succeed, celebrate their wins publicly. When they face setbacks, support them visibly.

Next we can create "sustainability sprints", where there will be focused periods where specific teams will tackle specific environmental challenges. If we want to change everything at a time those will be not manageable instead these small sprints target to do a chunk of job at a time. For example the packaging R&D team might find a proper solution for an alternative to plastic which is feasible for their product specifically then we can pass on the actual estimates, first batch etc to the management team. Or let's say a Procurement team dedicates a month on developing and teaching sustainable practices with local suppliers. Each sprint completed will build a good momentum and confidence.

Then we can implement something like "green shadowing", where the teams from different departments can experience the reality of how their decisions impact the environment. Like letting the finance teams visit the recycling facility or the product designers spend time with the feedback and response the customer care team got, these will allow us to know the gravity of a bad or good decision.

Now "feedback loops", we can improve at any point of time, but we need to measure things how well we have executed, like real time monitoring how much CO_2 is saved by choosing the January month decision? Are customers adapting with us? how much weekly waste reduction we have done, how with cumulative efforts we can manage to achieve a goal.

Now coming to the learning part we can name it "green learning journeys", structured programs, like a boot camp where teams can learn from other teams from other companies. By visiting their facility or factory we can see the actual solutions in action. Just imagine when a traditional manufacturer visits a zero waste facility or carbon neutral products, then impossible things feel possible.

To learn more and understand sustainability we can have "green mentorship" in today's world there are good sustainable consulting companies, where experienced sustainability practitioners will share how to start maybe or what things we are doing wrong. Their successfully led environmental initiatives can mentor a next generation manager.

Now finally, we need to think of "future back planning", like a clear vision of what actually we want us to see our company to be in 10 years, then work backward to identify baby steps that are needed today. When you see big MNCs are envisioning to be carbon neutral by 2030 or 2050, they actually map the quarterly steps that need to be followed to get there eventually.

These are not just strategies, they bridge across the chasm of change. Each one of the strategies addresses multiple barriers, the psychological resistance melts when people see success firsthand, organizational inertia weakens when change happens in focused sprints, short term thinking expands when metrics show possibilities.

The key is to start, no press conference, no grand occasion to start transformation, just we need to start. Every lesson learned becomes a stepping stone. The future of our planet depends on our skill in nurturing it, one deliberate action at a time.

Chapter 7

THE GREEN ORB: YOUR TURN

Vision of the Green Orb

I woke up and I could see the first rays of sun coming through the morning mist. I stand at the window to see the city wake up. It is not the city we know today, it is the dream we can create, the actual green city. And I can imagine the green orb not as a distant or long centuries dream, It is a reality that is waiting for us to unfold.

Imagine walking through urban streets, in the morning air, where the pm is under 50, carries the crisp of freshness my father and grandfather described from his childhood. Buildings are still touching the sky but they are now vertical forests, their facades alive with layering gardens that vibe with the breeze. These are not anymore decorative elements, they are living, creating systems that clean out the air, regulate proper temperature, and also a home for many insects, birds, etc. The concrete jungle is not transformed into a biodiverse paradise where nature and humans coexisted.

In this dream, businesses have changed. They have undergone a profound metamorphosis. The old smoke stacks which were once responsible for painting the skies with grey fumes have now been replaced by regenerative industrial parks, which operate just like our redwood forests. Here each and every company functions like a part of a larger ecosystem, where one company's waste becomes another's raw material. This creates a perfect circle of resource use. The quarterly reports now celebrate not just financial growth, but also the number of species returned to the area, the tons of carbon sequestered, and the communities enriched.

If we look up, we will see rooftops that tell their own stories of transformation. Solar panels are shining on every rooftop, smart windows adjust their transparency to get in more natural light, also big buildings are a part of mycorrhizal networks which regulate the temperature beneath these urban forest floors.

In our Green Orb, the invisible wall between industries and nature is no more. Today's manufacturing units operate like huge coral reefs, where every process supports the whole system. The supply chain is now more innovative with all the tech evolution we have gone through in this journey. Now the supply chain just flows like a river, no harm or CO2 involved in this process. Even these industries help more in creating positive waves.

The beautiful part of this vision is not the new innovation or architecture, it is the fundamental shift like how we perceive our role in the world. The language in the boardrooms has also been evolved, we can now hear more words like regeneration, stewardship etc. And we can see now more things are interconnected in our day to day life. For example the food on our plate tells the story of regenerative agriculture, where farms operate like prairies, building soil health while producing abundant harvests.

Also the clothes we wear which carry tags that now trace not just the origin but their environmental impact and step by step future recyclability. Every product is now designed with its entire lifecycle in mind, just like a small seed which has the blueprint for its whole existence, from a small sprout to a mature plant to create a better life for the next generation.

In this Green orb, global systems operate with harmony with nature's cycles. International trades flow like weather patterns maintaining a balance. Financial systems have evolved to recognize and reward the true value of natural capital, a healthy planet, nature is the only foundation of all wealth.

This may look like just another film set from the future but it is practical which is wrapped in an inspiring vision. Just like the first industrialists have imagined steam engines before they could build them, we all should envision a sustainable future before creating it. And this path if businesses follow then they can change the consumers and their mindset deeply. And just as my father shared his memories of clear skies and clean air, we now still have the opportunity to create new memories for future generations. Good memories, not of what was lost, but of what was gained when we chose to align our business practices with the wisdom of nature.

The Transformation Roadmap

So that now we know the Green Orb dream is nothing unreal, it is a journey that can start from today. Let's break down the whole journey into manageable stages.

Immediate Actions (0-1 Year): The Quantum Leap

- A thorough environmental audit, as we know we need to measure properly before treating them. Measure your carbon footprint, water usage, waste generation, and energy consumption.

- Basic implementations like, we can stop using single use plastic, follow basic recycling methods, and can stop using paper as much as possible, only digital reports, bills to reduce paper consumption (though emails, attachments, online things also generate carbon footprint but that's a broader part.)

- Then environmental intelligence systems should be there built in from the start of a new floor or any existing floors, like fire compliance and all other important compliances. AI powered sensors operations for HVAC systems, electricity consumption, for everything that is useful and possible.

- Then we can restructure the revenue streams the same as natural cycles. For example businesses can use their profitable seasons to fund their sustainable activities. Such as a beach hotel can use its peak summer profits to install renewable solutions during winter months.

- Now awareness programs, sustainable bootcamps, measurable targets we can focus on all levels at a company. And we can start transitioning to renewable energy sources, with a small change to a scaling up version.

Medium-Term Strategies (1-3 Years): The Symbiotic Shift

Like a young forest or the beginning of a new ecosystem, it starts creating its networks, in the medium term we need to strengthen and expand the initial efforts.

- There needs to be a positivity index ,where success can be measured in terms of reduction of natural harm ,biodiversity increase ,soil health improvement, air quality enhancement etc.

- We need to create waste processing systems that remove harmful materials and turn them into beneficial ones ,and then use that in another business or in general.

- There need to be business agreements which automatically adjust according to the environmental performance .Like partnering with suppliers or logistics who cause less harm to nature ,just like natural selection.

- Then with other companies we can start regenerative competition ,compete on metrics like" x tons of carbon sequestered "or" species diversity restored." Also there can be preferential access to sustainable financing and resources.

Long-Term Vision (5+ Years): The Conscious Corporation

Now here in this stage a lot of big companies are right now, this is where business surpasses its traditional boundaries to become something entirely new.

- At this point a company should be carbon neutral be it by 2030 or 2050 whatever. Align all the business cycles, operations, energy use, resource everything after thinking about nature first.

- As of today LLMs are getting more and more powerful, so we can expect this AI to go far beyond our expectations in a positive way and can develop AI systems that give your organization real time awareness of environmental impact across the whole company. Which is the same as how our bodies maintain homeostasis without conscious thought.

- We can create financial instruments that actually operate on principles of environmental uncertainty and interconnectedness.

- An unique way can be a reward system, there will be a global credit system like decentralized no one can regulate that except the companies who are participating in this. A "CC" Carbon Credit which will be given to the companies by achieving specific goals, which will definitely have value and companies can encash them and do whatever they want. One major point we can involve customers and everyone involved in the company. Just imagine in future the company's stock price is related to that CC (how powerful it will be).

- Finally a "regenerative manufacturing network". a company, a factory, an industry will be a self-sustaining ecosystem where waste powers communities, byproducts become new materials, and water returns cleaner than it arrived. Workers become environmental guardians, ensuring everything from heat to materials cycles endlessly, while products are designed for infinite life through repair and recycling.

And there are many more, one thing to remember this is not just for survival, it is about evolution. Every business, every system should need to be a conscious entity that will take care of nature.

Measuring Success

As we go forward to our green orb, yes I have told multiple times in this book but it is important without appreciation or support this can't be done. But we need to redefine the metrics of measuring success other than profit margins, market share, quarterly growth we need to think into a bit more depth.

Let's say we are doing good business, but we need to do the best business possible, and for that when we measure profit we need to measure the wealth of the soil beneath or the air quality around our operations, every aspect of nature that we touch in earning that profit. These all are more like a large tree's growth rings, where each circle tells a story about not just of growth, but of droughts weathered, nutrients absorbed, and seasons embraced.

The mathematics of this new success measurement is not complex, it is alive. Imagine counting the beats of a heart but not matching with the clock. We can measure success in breaths of fresh air that is added to the cities, in return the bird chirps in the industrial parks, urban areas will be a reward for us.

In this new change success can be measured in many layers, like the soil which has three main layers.

- **The surface layer/immediate impact:** daily operations that follow nature's rhythm

- **the middle layer/ecosystem enhancement:** strengthening nature's capacity to heal and grow more

- **the deep layer/generational impact:** a change which will be carried forward to the next generation; they will see this as this is the only reality.

This is not just a new way of measuring, it is a new way of seeing things, when we change what we measure, we change what we value. And when we change what we value, we change who we become. The true measure of success in our Green Orb will be stories that will pass generations. No I am not talking about generational wealth accumulated but stories of forests restored, waters cleaned, communities regenerated, and hope renewed. They matter in the world we are trying to create.

So the moral of the whole story is, measures need to be what we have given back to the nature that sustains us all.

Epilogue: The Green Orb in 2050

As I am writing these final words, my heart feels both heavy and hopeful. Yes heavy with the weight of what we have done to our only home, but also hopeful because I know we can do it, the path of giving our nature to heal. I find myself thinking about power sometimes, no not that power which runs machines, lights, etc, but the kind of power that shapes our future. The real power for the whole world lies not in destruction but in restoration, not about how much we can take or destroy but it is about how much we can protect and restore.

The COVID-19, yes that pandemic, has taught us a lot of unforgettable lessons. One of them is when the world paused, nature did not take our help to begin "healing." We have seen clear skies and clean water, etc but the deeper truth was more sobering. Research shows that the pandemic itself was a symptom of our broken trust with nature. Our relentless expansion into wild spaces, disruptions of the natural ecosystem, natural habitat, and our unsustainable resource use had created the perfect conditions for such a crisis. Our health and nature's health is connected in a way.

That global pause that I have felt in my lifetime forced us to confront another reality: Our businesses needed to fundamentally reimagine their relationship with nature, not only just adapt temporarily. Yes, there were immediate challenges and losses, but we understood one truth, no one is boss, our future prosperity depends not on dominating nature but on becoming stewards of it. The pandemic showed us that "building back better" meant building back in harmony with natural systems, understanding that public health, environmental health, and economic health are all threads of the same fabric.

Now as I dream of our world in 2050, I see that these lessons are fully realized by these homo sapiens. Let us imagine a day in this sustainable world we are creating ...

Yes a city is breathing the fresh air as the sun is rising. The morning air also carries the songs of birds that returned to urban forests which are growing vertically up building walls and also horizontally across the green corridors. People wake up to the natural light through the smart windows which also made HVAC systems outdated (we can see them in museums).

The morning commute is a rhythm of electric vehicles or hydrogen powered vehicles all powered by renewable energy. Also virtual offices blend seamlessly with physical spaces. In 2050, businesses are now integrated solely with this natural ecosystem. Manufacturing facilities are indistinguishable from forests, they now clean the air, purify water, and enhance biodiversity. Supply chains move like natural cycles, with materials flowing in continuous loops of reuse and renewal. Waste is an outdated concept, everything is a resource waiting for its next purpose.

The competition that once drove nations to build nuclear arsenals now they are restoring ecosystems. Yes we now compete for leadership in carbon sequestration, biodiversity enhancement, and environmental restoration. The new global superpowers are measured by wealth, military power but along with that they are measured by the health of their ecosystems and well-being of their people.

The rewards of this great leap are beyond what we have imagined. Yes we have achieved prosperity, but it's a prosperity that enriches rather than depletes. We have found security, but it is rooted in resilience rather than dominance. Compounding of our wealth now can be visible by visioning nature growing stronger.

As I look back from 2050, I can see that our greatest achievements were not technological or economic but also inherent and spiritual. This is our green orb, it began with small choices that grew into these transformative changes. And it is continuing.

The future is not something that happens to us but it is something we create with every choice we are making today. The green orb of 2050 is not waiting to be discovered or invented instead it is waiting to be built, one conscious decision at a time.

No constructive thing is easy. And so, dear reader as you close these pages, remember the power to create this future lies not is some distant technology or policy, but the choice we want to we chose to make today. The Green Orb is not just a destination, it is a journey we take together, step by step, choice by choice, toward a future where business and nature dance in perfect harmony.

The time to begin is now. The place to start is here businesses. The power to change lies within each of us.

Welcome to our Green Orb. Welcome home.

DISMANTLING FEW MYTHS
THAT CLOUD OUR GREEN VISION

Myth: "You need to sacrifice all the profits in the way of sustainability"

Reality:

- As of the 2018 report Unilever's sustainable living brands grew 69% faster than other portfolio products. This alone contributes to 75% of the company's growth. They have more than 28 sustainable living brands.

- Another research from McKinsey & Company shows that sustainability initiatives reduce costs through operational efficiencies (for example: waste reduction, energy savings).

Myth: "To follow the sustainability part a business needs overnight transformation"

Reality:

- For over a decade, Walmart has been working on sustainable improvements, gradually implementing solar energy, waste reduction, and sustainable sourcing.

- Most of the MNCs once started with small, clear goals of sustainability practices and then scaling up with time, like aiming for carbon neutrality or specific goals by 2030 or 2050.

Myth: "In huge industrial operations, renewable energy is unreliable"

Reality:

- Google has already achieved 100% renewable use in 2017 and they have more clear goals for the future. Just imagine how many users and data centers they have.

- The International Renewable Energy Agency (IRENA) states that the advancement in battery technology and smart grids makes renewable energy more reliable for industrial applications.

Myth: "Customers will not pay for sustainable products"

Reality:

- A 2020 IBM Consumer Survey shows that 57% of consumers are willing to change their shopping habits which will reduce the negative environmental impact.

- A recent Nielsen study shows that 73% of young global consumers are willing to pay more for the sustainable products.

Myth: "Sustainable practices are not for small businesses"

Reality:

- Many governments, organizations, NGO offers grants and incentives for small businesses to adopt sustainability.

- There are many brands globally, like Eco Femme (India), Allbirds (USA), and Mountain Rose Herbs (USA) prove that small businesses can afford sustainability while growing profitably.

Myth: "Product protection is compromised in sustainable packaging"

Reality:

- Over the years Nestlé has developed high-performance, recyclable, and biodegradable materials in packaging that ensure both safety and sustainability.

- The Sustainable Packaging coaliation reports shows that advances in biomaterials provide durability in comparison to plastic

Myth: "It is too expensive to construct Green buildings"

Reality:

- In the first 10 years, The Bullitt Center in Seattle generates 30% more energy than it has used.

- In Pune India Suzlon One Earth is a LEED Platinum certified campus that runs on renewable energy which reduces the long term operational cost.

Myth: "Recycling programs cost more and are also not worth it"

Reality:

- Coca Cola, one of the world's beverage company id investing in a circular economy. They are aiming to collect and recycle 100% of its packaging by 2030, reducing waste and costs.

- Studies have shown that recycled materials cost less than virgin materials in industries like aluminum and glass.

Myth: "Traditional industries can not be sustainable"

Reality:

- There is a steel giant named, ArcelorMittal that is investing in hyderogen based steel production, aim to cut CO2e drastically.

- The International Energy Agency (IEA) confirms that heavy industries can reduce huge amounts of emissions if they use clean energies.

Myth: "Sustainable practices only work in developed markets"

Reality:

- India's Godrej & Boyce is projecting 50% of its revenue from eco friendly products.

- Kenya's solar industry powers over 3 million homes, which makes them a renewable energy leader.

CARBON FOOTPRINT REDUCTION GUIDE: FROM QUICK WINS TO TRANSFORMATIVE IMPACT

Area	Low Effort Strategy	Approx CO2 reduction	High Impact Strategy	Approx CO2 reduction
Energy Management	Switch to LED lighting and smart sensors	15-20% reduction in lighting energy	Install on-site renewable energy (eg. solar + storage)	60-90% reduction in grid energy
Supply Chain	Optimize delivery routes and consolidate shipments	5-10% reduction in transport emissions	Restructure the supply chain to local/regional suppliers	40-60% reduction in logistics footprint

(contd.)

Waste Management	Implement recycling programs and paperless operations	10-15% reduction in waste emissions	Achieve zero waste to landfill through circular design	90-100% reduction in waste emissions
Building Operations	Install programmable thermostats and improve insulation	8-12% reduction in HVAC energy	Implement geothermal heating/ cooling systems	50-75% reduction in HVAC energy
Product Design	Use recycled packaging materials	5-15% reduction in product footprint	Redesign products for circularity and extended life	40-80% reduction in product lifecycle emissions
Water Systems	Install low-flow fixtures and leak detection	10-20% reduction in water-related energy	Implement water recycling and rainwater harvesting	70-90% reduction in water consumption energy
Employee Transport	Encourage remote work options	5-10% reduction in commuting emissions	Establish an electric fleet and charging infrastructure	50-70% reduction in fleet emissions
Data Centers	Optimize server utilization and cooling efficiency	15-25% reduction in IT energy	Relocate to renewable-powered regions with natural cooling	90-100% reduction in data center emissions
Manufacturing	Implement energy monitoring and equipment maintenance	10-15% reduction in production emissions	Transition to smart manufacturing with renewable power	60-80% reduction in manufacturing emissions

Materials Sourcing	Switch to recycled raw materials	10-20% reduction in material footprint	Develop bio-based alternatives and closed-loop systems	70-90% reduction in material emissions
Office Equipment	Enable power management features and energy-efficient settings	10-20% reduction in office equipment energy	Transition to cloud-based operations and thin clients	55-75% reduction in IT infrastructure emissions
Packaging Operations	Optimize package sizes and reduce void fill	8-15% reduction in packaging emissions	Develop reusable packaging systems and reverse logistics	60-80% reduction in packaging lifecycle emissions
Heating & Cooling Infrastructure	Install thermal window films and door seals	5-12% reduction in temperature control energy	Implement AI-driven smart building systems with heat recovery	45-65% reduction in climate control emissions
Warehouse Operations	Install motion-sensor lighting and optimize storage layout	12-18% reduction in warehouse energy	Implement automated storage and retrieval systems (ASRS) with renewable power	65-80% reduction in warehouse emissions
Marketing & Events	Switch to digital marketing and virtual product launches	20-30% reduction in marketing-related emissions	Develop carbon-neutral events and biodegradable promotional materials	85-95% reduction in event footprint

Few free resources by which businesses can start the journey.

Carbon & Energy Tools

EPA ENERGY STAR Portfolio Manager

Free building energy tracker, benchmarking tool, performance metrics, energy cost analysis, certification pathway

https://www.energystar.gov/buildings/benchmark

GHG Protocol Calculation Tools

Industry-standard emissions calculators, sector-specific guidance, scope 1-2-3 emissions tracking, reporting templates

https://ghgprotocol.org/calculation-tools-and-guidance

Carbon Footprint Calculator

Business carbon assessment, easy interface, downloadable reports, improvement recommendations

https://www.carbonfootprint.com/calculator.aspx

Resource Management

UN Global Compact Water Tool

Water risk assessment, usage tracking, conservation planning, regional water stress analysis

https://ceowatermandate.org/toolbox/

EPA WasteWise Program Tools

Waste reduction planning, materials tracking, cost savings calculator, waste audit templates

https://www.epa.gov/smm/wastewise-tools-and-resources

Assessment & Reporting

B Impact Assessment

Comprehensive sustainability assessment, benchmarking data, improvement tracking, stakeholder engagement tools

https://bimpactassessment.net/

Innovation Resources

Circular Economy Toolkit

Business model assessment, opportunity identification, implementation guides, case studies

https://circulareconomytoolkit.org/

Biomimicry Resource Handbook

Nature-inspired innovation tools, design principles, free educational resources, case examples

https://toolbox.biomimicry.org/

Planning & Strategy

SDG Action Manager

UN goals alignment, progress tracking, action planning, impact measurement

https://www.unglobalcompact.org/take-action/sdg-action-manager

Climate Toolkit

Climate strategy development, action planning, resource library, implementation guides

https://climateactiontoolkit.org/

REFERENCES

Chapter 1:

1. Carson, Rachel. "Silent Spring" (1962), Houghton Mifflin

2. Hawken, Paul. "The Ecology of Commerce" (2010), Harper Business

3. IPCC. "Climate Change 2023: Synthesis Report", Intergovernmental Panel on Climate Change

Chapter 2:

1. CDP Global Carbon Report 2023

2. International Energy Agency (IEA) World Energy Outlook 2023

3. World Resources Institute. "Global Carbon Budget 2023"

4. EPA. "Inventory of U.S. Greenhouse Gas Emissions and Sinks: 1990-2021"

5. McKinsey & Company. "Net-Zero Industry Tracker 2023"

Chapter 3:

1. Benyus, Janine. "Biomimicry: Innovation Inspired by Nature" (1997)

2. Wilson, Edward O. "The Diversity of Life" (1992), Harvard University Press

Chapter 4:

2. World Economic Forum. "The Global Risks Report 2023"

3. Polman, Paul. "Net Positive" (2021), Harvard Business Review Press

Chapter 5:

1. Bloomberg NEF. "New Energy Outlook 2023"

3. World Business Council for Sustainable Development Reports

4. Rocky Mountain Institute. "Annual Report 2023"

Chapter 6:

1. Kotter, John P. "Leading Change" (2012), Harvard Business Review Press

2. Thaler, Richard & Sunstein, Cass. "Nudge" (2021), Penguin Books

Chapter 7:

1. United Nations. "2030 Agenda for Sustainable Development"

3. Gates, Bill. "How to Avoid a Climate Disaster" (2021)

Key Data Sources & Organizations

1. Global Reporting Initiative (GRI)

2. Sustainability Accounting Standards Board (SASB)

3. Science Based Targets initiative (SBTi)

4. Task Force on Climate-related Financial Disclosures (TCFD)

5. CDP (formerly Carbon Disclosure Project)

6. United Nations Environment Programme (UNEP)

7. World Resources Institute (WRI)

8. International Renewable Energy Agency (IRENA)

ACKNOWLEDGMENTS

Every book is a journey, and no journey is completed alone. This work exists because of the unwavering support, guidance, and inspiration from many remarkable individuals who have touched my life in meaningful ways.

First and foremost, to my parents, my father, whose starlit conversations sparked the initial flame for this book, and my mother, whose endless encouragement and wisdom kept that flame burning bright. Your stories about how our world has changed over the decades became the foundation of my environmental consciousness. Thank you for teaching me to observe, question, and care deeply about our world.

To my teachers and mentors, who ignited my curiosity and guided me with patience and kindness. Your lessons went beyond textbooks; they shaped the way I see the world and inspired me to think critically and creatively.

To my friends and colleagues, who listened to my ideas, offered feedback, and supported me through this process. Your belief in this project kept me going.

And finally, to nature itself, our greatest teacher. Thank you for showing us, through millions of years of evolution, that sustainability isn't just an option; it's the only way forward.

I am deeply grateful to everyone who has been part of this journey.

ABOUT THE AUTHOR

Anindita Ghosh is a Business Management graduate specializing in Marketing from XIM, School of Commerce (Xavier University Bhubaneswar). Currently working as a Marketing Associate and she also helps in her family business. She is trying to understand how businesses can work better with nature and not going against it. While gaining practical experience in the field, she is also preparing for higher education in business.

Her book, "My Dream Green Orb: Where Business Meets the Planet's Needs", comes from stories her father, mother and grandparents shared about a green lively nature and her simple understanding of business. Though she does not have years of experience she hopes to add a fresh perspective to the conversation about how businesses play a crucial role in protecting our environment.

When not working, Anindita spends time in her small garden, does painting, reads books, practice calligraphy, or capture moments of nature. She also loves to travel occasionally which helps her see both the simple beauty of nature and how much we need to protect it.

It is her first attempt of writing a book, she hopes her thoughts might help add something useful to the conversation about doing business and focusing on environment sustainability (putting nature first always).

Scan to step into our interactive Green Orb. Also, share your sustainable journey and feedback.

End of the Book